WISE SAYINGS

of

THE

CELTS

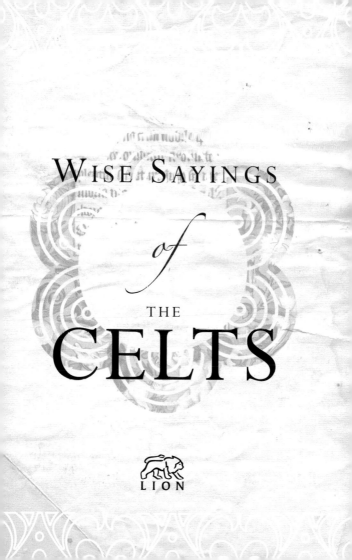

WISE SAYINGS

of

THE

CELTS

LION

Compiled by Andrea Skevington
This edition copyright © 2012 Lion
Hudson

The author asserts the moral right
to be identified as the author of this
work

A Lion Book
an imprint of
Lion Hudson plc
Wilkinson House, Jordan Hill Road,
Oxford OX2 8DR, England
www.lionhudson.com
ISBN 978 0 7459 5569 8

Distributed by:
UK: Marston Book Services, PO Box
269, Abingdon, Oxon, OX14 4YN
USA: Trafalgar Square Publishing, 814
N. Franklin Street, Chicago, IL 60610
USA Christian Market: Kregel
Publications, PO Box 2607, Grand
Rapids, Michigan 49501

First edition 2012
10 9 8 7 6 5 4 3 2 1 0

A catalogue record for this book is
available from the British Library

Typeset in 11.5/12 Perpetua and
10/24 Zapfino

Printed and bound in China

ACKNOWLEDGMENTS

BACKGROUNDS

iStock: Jussi Santaniemi

ILLUMINATED MANUSCRIPTS

Corbis: Fine Art Photographic Library

MOTIFS

iStock: Jamie Farrant, Liudmilla
Chernova, Rusanovska

PHOTOGRAPHS

Corbis: pp. 8–9, 15 Homer Sykes;
pp. 52–53 Ashley Cooper

iStock: pp. 6–7 tirc83; pp. 10, 26–27
Jon Helgason; p. 13 Gord Horne;
pp. 18–19, 46–47 Christian Keller;
pp. 20–21 thefurnaceroom; pp. 25,
35 Andy Dean; pp. 29, 34 Donall O
Cleirigh; pp. 30–31 Peter Zelei;
pp. 38–39 Lisa Ison; p. 41 Gene Lee;
pp. 42–43 Amanda Witt; p. 44 Stacy
Able; pp. 50–51 Kit Sen Chin;
pp. 58–59 Nicholas Belton

COVER

Background: Jussi Santaniemi/
iStock

Illuminated manuscript:
The Gallery Collection/Corbis

Photograph: andipantz/iStock

ONTENTS

INTRODUCTION

Our age is rediscovering the ancient wisdom of the Celts, and finding that their words speak powerfully into our modern world. Their love of nature and their deep spirituality remind us to take time to be still, and to know the presence of God in our daily routines.

This book brings together many beautiful writings: still fresh though centuries old, and more recent but full of ancient wisdom. These poems, stories, and meditations are a delight.

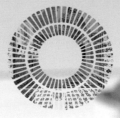

meditation

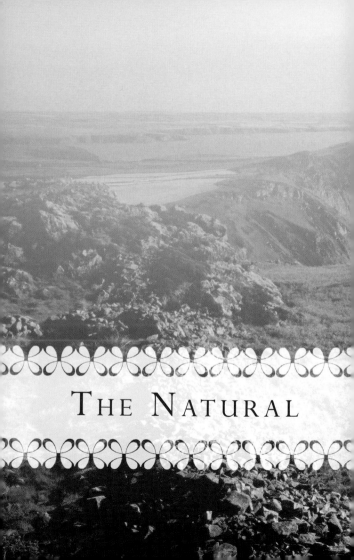

THE NATURAL

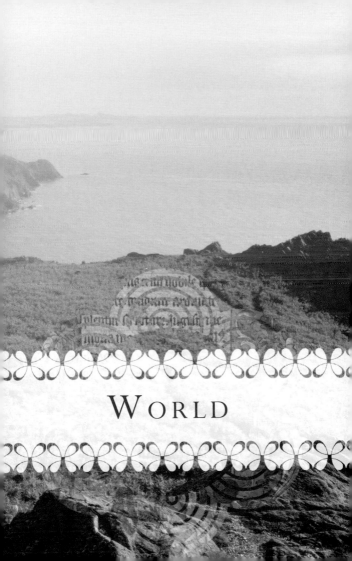

WORLD

Deep peace of the running wave to you.
Deep peace of the flowing air to you.
Deep peace of the quiet earth to you.
Deep peace of the shining stars to you.
Deep peace of the infinite peace to you.

ADAPTED FROM ANCIENT GAELIC RUNES

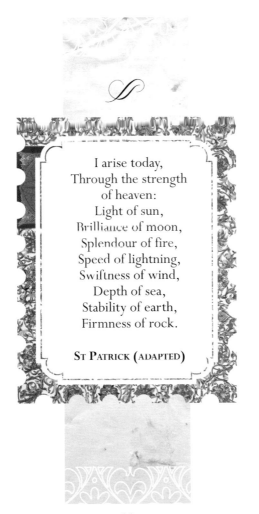

I arise today,
Through the strength
of heaven:
Light of sun,
Brilliance of moon,
Splendour of fire,
Speed of lightning,
Swiftness of wind,
Depth of sea,
Stability of earth,
Firmness of rock.

ST PATRICK (ADAPTED)

Almighty Creator, who hast made all things,
The world cannot express all thy glories,
Even though the grass and the trees
should sing.

The Father has wrought so great a
multitude of wonders
That they cannot be equalled.
No letters can contain them,
no letters can express them.

He who made the wonder of the world
Will save us, has saved us.
It is not too great toil to praise the Trinity.

Purely, humbly, in skilful verse
I should delight to give praise to the Trinity.

It is not too great toil to praise the Son
of Mary.

WELSH POEM

O Son of the living God, old eternal King,
I desire a hidden hut in the wilderness that it
may be my home.

A narrow little blue stream beside it and a clear
pool for the washing away of sin through the
grace of the Holy Ghost.

A lovely wood close about it on every side,
to nurse birds with all sorts of voices and to hide
them with its shelter.

Looking south for heat, and a stream through its
land, and good fertile soil suitable for all plants.

A beautiful draped church, a home for God
from Heaven, and bright lights above the clean
white Gospels.

Enough of clothing and food from the King
of fair fame, and to be sitting for a while and
praying to God in every place.

ST MANCHON (ATTRIBUTED)

At one Lenten season, St Kevin, as was his way, fled from the company of men to a certain solitude, and in a little hut that did but keep out the sun and the rain, gave himself earnestly to reading and to prayer, and his leisure to contemplation alone. And as he knelt in his accustomed fashion, with his hand outstretched through the window and lifted up to heaven, a blackbird settled on it, and busying herself as in her nest, laid in it an egg. And so moved was the saint that in all patience and gentleness he remained, neither closing nor withdrawing his hand: but until the young ones were fully hatched he held it out unwearied, shaping it for the purpose.

GERALD OF WALES

solitude

S

The woodland thicket overtops me,
the blackbird sings me a lay, praise I will not conceal:
above my lined little booklet
the thrilling of birds sings to me.

The clear cuckoo sings to me, lovely discourse,
in its grey cloak from the crest of the bushes;
truly – may the Lord protect me! –
well do I write under the forest wood.

TAKEN FROM STUDIES IN EARLY CELTIC NATURE POETRY

Delightful would it be to me to be in Ulster
  On the pinnacle of a rock,
That I might often see
  The face of the ocean;
That I might see its heaving waves
  Over the wide ocean,
When they chant music to their Father
  Upon the world's course;
That I might see its level sparkling strand,
  It would be no cause of sorrow;
That I might hear the song of the wonderful bar
  Source of happiness;
That contrition might come upon my heart
  Upon looking at her …

That I might bewail my evils all,
  Though it were difficult to compute them;
That I might bless the Lord
  Who conserves all,
Heaven with its countless bright orders,
Land, strand and flood.

St Columba

I am the wind which breathes upon the sea,
I am the wave of the ocean,
I am the murmur of the billows,
I am the ox of the seven combats,
I am the vulture upon the rocks,
I am a beam of the sun,
I am the fairest of plants,
I am a wild boar in valour,
I am a salmon in the water,
I am a lake in the plain,
I am a word of science,
I am the point of the lance of battle,
I am the God who creates in the head the fire.

THE MYSTERY OF AMERGIN

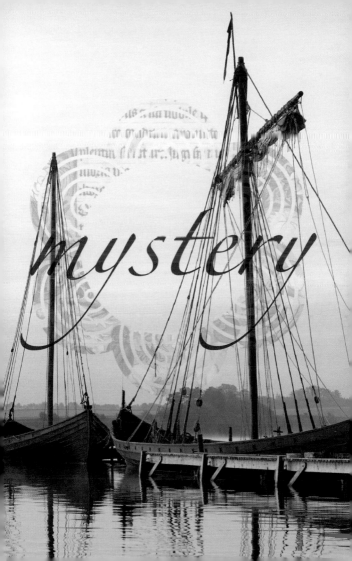

mystery

THE DAILY

ROUND

I arise today
Through God's strength to pilot me:
God's might to uphold me,
God's wisdom to guide me,
God's eye to look before me,
God's ear to hear me,
God's word to speak for me,
God's hand to guard me,
God's way to lie before me,
God's shield to protect me,
God's host to save me.

St Patrick

Thanks to thee, O God, that I have
    risen today,
To the rising of this life itself;
May it be to Thine own glory, O God
    of every gift,
And to the glory of my soul likewise.

O great God, aid Thou my soul
With the aiding of Thine own mercy;
Even as I clothe my body with wool,
Cover Thou my soul with the shadow
    of Thy wing.

Help me to avoid every sin,
And of every sin to forsake;
And as the mist scatters on the crest
    of the hills,
May each ill haze clear from my soul,
    O God.

CARMINA GADELICA (ADAPTED)

I will kindle my fire this morning
In the presence of the holy angels of heaven,
In the presence of Ariel of the loveliest form,
In the presence of Uriel of the myriad charms,
Without malice, without jealousy, without envy,
Without fear, without terror of any one under the sun,
But the Holy Son of God to shield me.

God, kindle Thou in my heart within
A flame of love to my neighbour,
To my foe, to my friend, to my kindred all,
To the brave, to the knave, to the thrall,
O Son of the loveliest Mary,
From the lowliest thing that liveth,
To the Name that is highest of all.

CARMINA GADELICA (ADAPTED)

Let me bless almighty God,
whose power extends over sea and land,
whose angels watch over all.

Let me study sacred books to calm my soul:
I pray for peace,
kneeling at heaven's gates.

Let me do my daily work,
gathering seaweed, catching fish,
giving food to the poor.

Let me say my daily prayers,
sometimes chanting, sometimes quiet,
always thanking God.

Delightful it is to live
on a peaceful isle, in a quiet cell,
serving the King of kings.

St Columba

I arise today
Through the strength of the love
of the Cherubim,
In obedience of angels,
In the service of archangels,
In the hope of resurrection to
meet with reward,
In prayers of patriarchs,
In prediction of prophets,
In preaching of apostles,
In faith of confessions,
In innocence of holy virgins,
In deeds of righteous men.

ST PATRICK

heaven

At Tara to-day in this fateful hour
I place all Heaven with its power,
And the sun with its brightness,
And the snow with its whiteness,
And the fire with all the strength it hath,
And the lightning with its rapid wrath,
And the winds with their swiftness along their path,
And the sea with its deepness,
And the rocks with their steepness,
And the earth with its starkness
    All these I place,
      By God's almighty help and grace,
Between myself and the powers of darkness.

THE RUNE OF ST PATRICK

SLEEPING PRAYER

I am placing my soul and my body
On Thy sanctuary this night, O God,
On Thy sanctuary, O Jesus Christ,
On Thy sanctuary, O Spirit of perfect truth;
    The Three who would defend my cause,
    Nor turn Their backs upon me.

Thou, Father, who art kind and just,
Thou, Son, who didst overcome death,
Thou, Holy Spirit of power,
Be keeping me this night from harm;
    The Three who would justify me
    Keeping me this night and always.

CARMINA GADELICA

soul and

body

DARKNESS

AND LIGHT

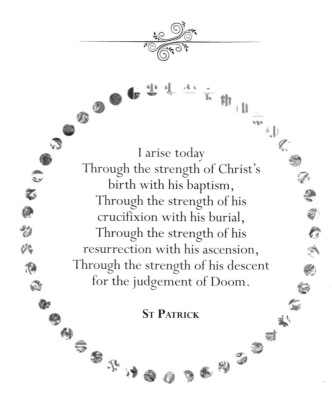

I arise today
Through the strength of Christ's
birth with his baptism,
Through the strength of his
crucifixion with his burial,
Through the strength of his
resurrection with his ascension,
Through the strength of his descent
for the judgement of Doom.

St Patrick

You are the peace of all things calm
You are the place to hide from harm
You are the light that shines in dark
You are the heart's eternal spark
You are the door that's open wide
You are the guest who waits inside
You are the stranger at the door
You are the calling of the poor
You are my Lord and with me still
You are my love, keep me from ill
You are the light, the truth, the way
You are my Saviour this very day.

CELTIC ORAL TRADITION

Be thou my vision,
O Lord of my heart,
Naught be all else to me,
Save that thou art;
Be thou my best thought
In the day and the night,
Both waking and sleeping,
Thy presence my light.

DALLAN FORGAILL (ATTRIBUTED)

Kindle in our hearts, O God,
The flame of that love which never ceases,
That it may burn in us, giving light to others.
May we shine forever in Thy holy temple,
Set on fire with Thy eternal light,
Even Thy son, Jesus Christ,
Our Saviour and Redeemer.

PRAYER OF ST COLUMBA OF IONA

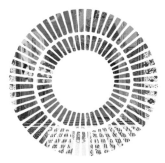

O God, who broughtest me
from the rest of last night
Unto the joyous light of this day,
Be Thou bringing me from
the new light of this day
Unto the guiding light
of eternity.
Oh! from the new light
of this day
Unto the guiding light
of eternity.

CARMINA GADELICA

As the rain hides the stars,
as the autumn mist hides the hills,
as the clouds veil the blue of the sky,
so the dark happenings of my lot
hide the shining of your face from me.

Yet, if I may hold your hand in the darkness,
it is enough, since I know that,
though I may stumble in my going,
you do not fall.

CELTIC PRAYER

SETH:

Cherub, angel of the God of grace,
In the tree I saw,
   High up on the branches,
A little child newly born;
And he was swathed in cloths,
   And bound fast with napkins.

grace

CHERUBIN:

The Son of God it was whom thou sawest,
Like a little child swathed.
    He will redeem Adam, thy father,
With his flesh and blood too,
When the time is come,
    And thy mother, and all the good people.

He is the oil of mercy,
    Which was promised to thy father;
Through his death, clearly,
    All the world will be saved.

FROM AN ANCIENT CORNISH DRAMA,
THE VISION OF SETH

My dear sister, there is an ocean of
happiness prepared for us; and what we
experience here is but a drop, or a taste
of that which we shall enjoy.
A sight of his love is the cause of our
love; and our thirst after him is but
the effect of his thirst after us; and our
diligence in seeking of him is the effect
of his diligence in seeking of us.

FROM A LETTER OF PANTYCELYN

thirst

GOD WITH US

men are blind,
ack knowledge,
all mute dogs,

I met a stranger yest're'een;
I put food in the eating place,
Drink in the drinking place,
Music in the listening place;
And, in the sacred name of the Triune,
He blessed myself and my house,
My cattle and my dear ones,

And the lark said in her song,
    Often, often, often,
Goes the Christ in the stranger's guise;
    Often, often, often,
Goes the Christ in the stranger's guise.

A Scottish hospitality prayer

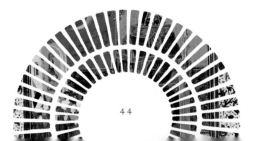

I find that the Lord Jesus
is as a golden mine in our
own fields, under our own
earth, and is in Saints as
the soul in the eye, or Sun
in the Firmament, or fire
in the inward furnace, or
inhabitant in a house.

MORGAN LLWYD

Lord, Thou art my island; in Thy bosom I rest.
Thou art the calm of the sea; in that peace I stay.
Thou art the deep waves of the shining ocean.
With their eternal sound I sing.
Thou art the song of the birds; in that tune is my joy.
Thou art the smooth white strand of the shore;
in Thee is no gloom.
Thou art the breaking of the waves on the rock;
Thy praise is echoed in the swell.
Thou art the Lord of my life.

PRAYER OF ST COLUMBA OF IONA

God to enfold me,
God to surround me,
God in my speaking,
God in my thinking.

God in my sleeping,
God in my waking,
God in my watching,
God in my hoping.

God in my life,
God in my lips,
God in my soul,
God in my heart.

God in my suffering,
God in my slumber,
God in mine ever-living soul,
God in mine eternity.

CARMINA GADELICA (ADAPTED)

watching

My Christ! my Christ! my shield, my encircler,
Each day, each night, each light, each dark:
   My Christ! my Christ! my shield, my encircler,
   Each day, each night, each light, each dark.

Be near me, uphold me, my treasure, my triumph,
In my lying, in my standing, in my watching,
   in my sleeping,

Jesus, Son of Mary! my helper, my encircler,
Jesus, Son of David! my strength everlasting:
   Jesus, Son of Mary! my helper, my encircler,
   Jesus, Son of David! my strength everlasting.

ENCOMPASSING PRAYER

I' arise today
Through a mighty strength:
God's power to guide me,
God's might to uphold me,
God's eyes to watch over me;
God's ear to hear me,
God's word to give me speech,
God's hand to guard me,
God's way to lie before me,
God's shield to shelter me,
God's host to secure me.

BRIGID OF GAEL

Christ with me, Christ before me, Christ behind me,
Christ in me, Christ beneath me, Christ above me,
Christ on my right, Christ on my left,
Christ when I lie down, Christ when I sit down,
Christ when I arise,
Christ in the heart of every man who thinks of me,
Christ in the mouth of everyone who speaks of me,
Christ in every eye that sees me,
Christ in every ear that hears me.

ST PATRICK (ADAPTED)

heart

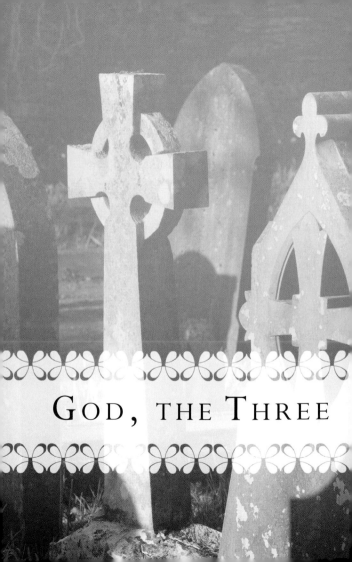

GOD, THE THREE

IN ONE

In the name of Father,
In the name of Son,
In the name of Spirit,
Three in One:

Father cherish me,
Son cherish me,
Spirit cherish me,
Three all-kindly.

God make me holy,
Christ make me holy,
Spirit make me holy,
Three all-holy.

Three aid my hope,
Three aid my love,
Three aid mine eye,
And my knee from stumbling,
My knee from stumbling.

Carmina Gadelica

*I rise today
in the power's strength,
invoking the Trinity
believing in threeness,
confessing the oneness,
of creation's Creator.*

ST PATRICK

With God be my walking this day,
With Christ be my walking this day,
With Spirit my walking this day,
The Threefold all-kindly my way:
Ho, ho, ho! The Threefold all-kindly I pray.

My shielding this day be from bane,
My shielding this night be from pain,
Ho! Ho! soul and body, the twain,
By Father, Son, Spirit, amain;
By Father's, by Son's, and by Holy Ghost's sain.

The Father be he shielding me,
And be God the Son shielding me,
The Spirit be he shielding me,
As Three and as One let them be:
Ho, ho, ho! as Three and as One Trinity.

POEMS OF THE WESTERN HIGHLANDERS

Bless, O Threefold true and bountiful,
Myself, my spouse, and my children,
My tender children and their beloved mother at their head.
On the fragrant plain, on the gay mountain sheiling,
On the fragrant plain, on the gay mountain sheiling.

Everything within my dwelling or in my possession,
All kine and crops, all flocks and corn,
From Hallow Eve to Beltane Eve,
With goodly progress and gentle blessing,
From sea to sea, and every river mouth,
From wave to wave, and base of waterfall.

Be the Three Persons taking possession of all
to me belonging,
Be the sure Trinity protecting me in truth;
Oh! satisfy my soul in the words of Paul,
And shield my loved ones beneath the wing of Thy glory,
Shield my loved ones beneath the wing of Thy glory.

CARMINA GADELICA

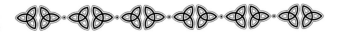

Be the eye of God dwelling with you,
The foot of Christ in guidance with you,
The shower of the Spirit pouring on you,

Richly and generously.

PRAYER FOR PROTECTION

Richly

BIBLIOGRAPHY

A M Allchin and Esther de Waal, eds., *Threshold of Light*, London: Darton, Longman and Todd, 1986.
David Adam, *The Cry of the Deer*, London: Triangle / SPCK, 1987.
Alexander Carmichael, *Carmina Gadelica: Hymns and Incantations*, Edinburgh: Floris Books, 1992.
E A Sharp and J Matthay, eds., *Lyra Celtica: An Anthology of Representative Celtic Poetry*, London: John Grant, 1924.

WEBSITES:
www.amaranthpublishing.com – Amaranth Publishing
www.allsaintsbrookline.org/celtic – All Saints Parish, Brookline
www.faithandworship.org – Faith and Worship
www.franciscanponderings.blogspot.com – Franciscan Ponderings
www.worldprayers.org – The World Prayers Project